Aden Rolfe | False Nostalgia

New Poems

GIRAMONDO POETS

Aden Rolfe | False Nostalgia

First published 2016
from the Writing & Society Research Centre
at Western Sydney University
by the Giramondo Publishing Company
PO Box 752 Artarmon NSW 1570 Australia
www.giramondopublishing.com

Designed by Harry Williamson
Typeset by Andrew Davies
in 10/16.5 pt Baskerville

Printed and bound by Ligare
Distributed in Australia by NewSouth Books

National Library of Australia
Cataloguing-in-Publication data:

Rolfe, Aden
False Nostalgia / Aden Rolfe

ISBN 978-1-922146-99-1 (pbk)
A821.4

for Claire

I'm looking forward to the
memories of right now
DRAKE

the picture is cut up not only into inert, formless elements
containing little information or signifying power, but
also into falsified elements, carrying false information
GEORGES PEREC

Contents

Anamnesis

Ars memoria

Anamnesis

Anamnesis

We are who we are because of
what we remember—

how warm it was on the way out
to the lake
the shade of grey gums and weatherboard houses

water that wanted us to walk
around it, to swallow the
stones we failed to skim across.
We stuttered there
in irony and earnest
wanting to say *I love you*
even though we couldn't
and shouldn't have.

The problem, in both love and language
is not sincerity.

When our memories change
    so do our stories

                                        one thing leading
to another, moments reconfigured
to maintain the narrative. For instance

when we came back from the lake again
found that goat on the driveway.

They say just because something happens
doesn't make it meaningful. That it
could've happened differently.
That it probably did.

That's why I keep replaying the scene
wondering if I should call
clarify my position.

I remember you saying you wanted
new structures of thought
                the banks a little dry
    a little out of breath, enough

to suggest the edge
                        and its possibilities.

If these are the moments that make up a life
what does it mean to hold back?

In the meantime, the parts
come together, give the impression of
a continuous whole

everything set in a landscape
real and imagined encounters
with ourselves and others.

Lakes understand mystery
better than narrative, self-
containment preferable

to an open system

to slipping under the surface.
Even still

the best moments occur in these
spaces

    coastlines and beaches
    clearings and trails.

The details change in the telling
but something invariably
floats to the top.
 The goat.
 The driveway.
 The artist's
impression of a train station, me
sizing up my reflection, you
with your briefcase
        no knees
            blurred face.

They say memories don't disappear
they just need the right cue, the way
                                                            light rain

recalls that Japanese temple. It was
inside a shed
            on which
they'd painted
an image of the temple. To know
who we are, they say
we need to know who we were

but I couldn't find the files
       no longer sure
where to look.

No one saw the temple, no one
       saw the shed.

I remember you wanted
a range of values
not definitive states.

I remember reading on the train, then counting
houses by the lake
in the pulse of cicadas.

I remember being told that these are what
our stories are made of

the moments we choose to hold on to.

They say forgetting is a function of time.

When our stories change
so do our lives
continuity an illusion
to pull us through.

They say we can never really know how it happened
or who we were, only
that it happened differently
whether we come to it on a quiet night
or in clear, dry mountain air.

Forgetting lets us fashion
a coherent picture—

the stuttering edge
the slipping surface
    the trees out of breath.

We recast ourselves
let the picture develop.
The plot accommodates.

They say we're plural, post-memory
too old not to know

we should be playing *what when*
instead of
          what if.

Choices branch into possible presents
but it's the rest of the time

when the relation between action and outcome
is uncertain, when the world doesn't quite
   cohere

          those are the moments
that make up a life.

          They say that just
          because it's meaningful
     doesn't mean it happened.

So find your mark
look across the lake.

If you can't manage a good shot
just take what you can get.

Cherry Blossom

Cherry blossom is enough. Plum blossom is too far. The woods wet and not quite real, breathe us out for want of breadcrumbs. That little bird, I presume, that little bird wandered in and ate them. This is not a koan, he said, and then words we wanted to say, like 'throat' and 'nostril'. The sound of thunder clapping. A tin of quail eggs and other dishes best served cold. Would I could I drink from the stream once more with you, reflection. If only to unlend you that money. Ruptured by rain, the last thing you said: Moss knows no difference between a rock submerged and an exposed shoulder. Or was it algae? The details are lost and what remains is a shared history of suggestion. We can't know which way the water flowed, except 'toward the sea' which was anyone's guess.

Meridian

Catalogue everything in the garden
by outlook and trope. Both daylight and
shoulders can be broad

remember, but are leaves defined by veins
or diameter? How many stones are left
unturned? And which things are not things
apart from holes and shade?

If the eye connects points in space
we know it's the vector that defines
                                        where we are
and where to from here.

Walk the perimeter, it says. Think your way
toward the moment. Beneath the grass
            a dynamic play of boundary and shape.

Exchanges

for Martin Harrison

We expected more from the twenty-first
century. Some direction, some push, some instruction
for living in the present-continuous. A cure for boredom
perhaps, self-annihilating or otherwise. Instead we set the scene
take the photo, update our statuses.

    I should've answered your question with a question, I realise
with the same question, but the words escaped me
filled the car like so much regret, forcing us
onto the side of the road, somewhere near
______. We stood and looked at it awhile
menacing like a wasp nest, bloated with thought. It was
neveralways phatic with you, but alwaysnever
a broken fiction, ready to shift unexpectedly
like sunsets on towers of hubris, stalling things
for a while. And later, night roads in monochrome, dawdling into
another year, at least until we knew what to do. But at this moment
I can't help think: what is hope predicated on, exactly, what are
its prompts? And in their absence, then what? In the face
of the babble and chatter, of the *excellents* and *hahaha awesomes*
would you even hear it intoning: interesting, interesting
    yes
interesting? We're all polysemic
but approval means more when it's conditional.

Meanwhile, just outside of shot
the runner has arrived with iced tea and a jam donut and
a list of things, thingness things, things I forgot to ask, now being
the time of inquiry, ______ being the place of inquiry.
I'll forget them again no doubt, I've forgotten them
already, lost the slips of paper I wrote them down on. I'll
have to look them up again, ask you againagain, walk them into
being. Eventually, the pebblecrete palace and its seagullsurrounded
tower, visible from the farthest corners of this city
will cease to matter, along with plans, and ideas
and where you were until now. We know what we face
in uncertainty, it's a path laid out to escape oneself.
But it's gone now, with the times, it's gone
and returned.

What have you been up to

I was worried about something
I just can't remember what it was

no matter
we go jogging along the water

down to the park
under the viaduct by the canal

great places
to commit crimes or uncover them

which is what it comes down to   really
discrete goals   ritual and activity
progression and reversion

good habits are not   their own reward
and the idea of experiencing something
in the moment still draws us in

even if we have difficulty
imagining things that are not present

still   nothing is happening
and if someone were to ask what we've been up to
we'd have little to report

stuck on the outside track
unsure who's speaking
never mind who's at the centre

but one day you'll find a lump
with searching fingers

you'll change your health cover
at last come to appreciate
the things you can't buy your way out of

which is the dawning realisation
of our time

and on a night
not far from now
you'll find yourself
by the expressway

a little lost
too much money in your pocket
to get an engaged tone
or to see a car slowing down

but for now
nothing is happening

nothing happened
nothing is going to happen

we'll start jogging again
be tempted to jump in the harbour with the dogs
think better of it
go on as before

Afterthoughts

Mark a sentence with your finger, draw a line
in the dirt. You say that if you look to your endpoint
and not at what you're doing, you'll miss your stop.
It's too dark to read, though, and I'm less asleep
than I ought to be. We stand awhile, just listening—
back-of-the-neck prickles presaging a storm.
Remember, a cough is a speech-act
a pause is a thoughtform and only the water
knows the moon is blind. So cast your mind back
to when, float up to describe the parallels. We all
want something, even just to meet at infinity.
If you watch your hand as you draw, I say
you'll find your mark by a curved path. You consider this
a moment, breathe on your coffee
                                        call me a liar.

We Watched the Waves

get out your map and compass
stay the morning with an out-turned palm
these are the days we'll look back on and say
do you remember the time
in the
house by the
beach?
we need to act now
do something

here   i'll stuff a pigeon in a bottle
and set it out to sea
but the message stays the same
have you ever known solitude?

at low tide we hold shells to our ears   strain to hear
the water for the sea
the important thing is to keep moving   stay warm
chase the seagulls   you know they'd do the same for you

maybe you should learn the clarinet   but do it after lunch
else whose washing am i hanging out?
don't mention the waves   you never know what'll come back

you heard i traded all my stories for seed packets
some grew   some didn't
mint or basil   tomato or jalapeño
by spring   pesto or salsa
though which we can't say

i admit it now   emptying my shoe   i've never
really known solitude
i even drove round all night looking for it

tie a key to a kitestring   just so something
for once   will happen

a late afternoon indistinctness set in
the sand greyer outside photographs
and though alanna brought her pencils
and offered to make some adjustments

i was already knee-deep in dune grass
if we could start again   wake up just a little earlier
we try to watch the waves so that later we can say
we watched the waves
but vertigo takes hold
neither of us trusts the other
not to simply wander in

A note on 'We Watched the Waves'

I won't remember doing it, but no doubt I'm copying out the words—*we watched the waves*—because they strike something in me.

> Still later, on the beach, we watched the waves.
> No two the same size. No two in the same arch
> of rising up and pouring. But it is the same law.
>
> (Robert Hass, 'On Squaw Peak')

In another poem, 'The Dry Mountain Air', Hass provides a two-page account of visits from his extravagant grandmother. Each time she would arrive in a limousine, carefully remove her hat 'as if it were a nest / Of fledgling birds' and present Hass and his brother with gifts. He closes the poem:

> My brother, four years older,
> Says this never happened. Not once. She never visited the house
> On Jackson Street with its sea air and the sound of fog horns
> At the Gate. I thought it might help to write it down here
> That the truth of things might be easier to come to
> On a quiet evening in the clear, dry, mountain air.

Hass' whole recollection, with its images of chocolate and pearl-grey gloves and whiffs of anise, turns, according to his brother, on a false memory. The poem is his attempt to come to terms with the difference between what he remembers and what really happened.

A false memory is a memory of something that didn't happen to you but which you remember as if it had. It occurs when a secondary memory—something experienced by someone else, something you're told about, something you invent—becomes a primary one—something you believe happened to you—by losing the source or confusing the particulars. We unconsciously alter the details and an imaginary episode is transformed into a remembered one.

The same process underpins what Oliver Sacks calls 'cryptomnesia', a kind of unconscious plagiarism where you mistake a received idea for an original thought.

Like Hass, Sacks has had his memory corrected by an older sibling. In his memoir, *Uncle Tungsten*, he lucidly recounts a bombing incident during the Blitz. But upon reading this account, his brother Michael remarks, simply, 'You never saw it. You weren't there.' They were both at boarding school at the time, apparently, away from London. Sacks had appropriated the episode from a letter. As with false memories, cryptomnesia occurs when the source of the information gets misplaced in your mental filing system: you remember the details, just not where they came from. There's also 'autoplagiarism', where you rehash or reproduce ideas of your own as if they were fresh thoughts. The only way you find out if you're copying yourself is if you have some record of it, if you come across your words in an old notebook or stumble upon them in an old poem.

According to Plato, we forget both the details and the sources of the knowledge we've acquired in past lives at the moment we are born. Learning, then, is not how we gain new knowledge from without, but how we recover old knowledge from within. His name for this kind of recollection, this coming to knowledge, is *anamnesis*.

You negotiate your position in relation to an event, particularly an emotionally resonant one, through memory. This affects not only that event and that specific memory, but your relation to the larger whole; that is, how you moderate your identity in relation to the world.

We hold on to these memories through stories. As Sacks notes elsewhere, 'We have each of us a life-story, an inner narrative whose continuity, whose sense is our lives.' This narrative maintains your sense of self, linking who you are in the present instant with who you were in the moment prior, and the moment before that. We construct this autobiography 'continually, unconsciously, by, through, and in us—through our perceptions, our feelings, our thoughts, our actions; and, not least, our discourse, our spoken narrations.'

This process of revising our lives is summarily described by Italo Calvino in his novel *Mr Palomar*:

> A person's life consists of a collection of events, the last of which could also change the meaning of the whole, not because it counts more than the previous ones but because once they are included in a life, events are arranged in an order that is not chronological but, rather, corresponds to an inner architecture.

We don't invent this inner architecture from nothing. Rather, we exist in a narrative framework that determines the form of our storytelling and the way it organises memory. Language establishes the set of relations for arranging and conveying the events of your life, allowing you to recall the individual parts of different episodes. When Proust's (thinly) fictional stand-in, Marcel, bites into the madeleine, he reaches for language to provide a shape to the sensation, to resolve it in terms he can retain for his own benefit and relay to us for ours. The cake offers him continuity between his childhood self and his adult persona, and writing it down provides him the ability to access, at will, not the sensation itself, but the experience of it. Through narrative he transforms an involuntary memory, dependant on taste, into a voluntary one, available at a whim.

But just as dipping a cake in tea alters its taste and texture, placing a memory in a narrative changes its essence. The storied memory doesn't cease to be true (if it was true to begin with) but comes to be a representation of its real-world counterpart rather than its equivalent. It hovers between true and false, at the service not of itself, but of the telling. It's necessarily incomplete, a version of what happened in the context of what might have happened. Your autobiography, then, becomes a theory of your life, not a proof.

All stories privilege some details over others, and this one is no different. I've put everything in an order that reflects not the fragmentary nature of memory, but one that follows a narrative logic.

'The Western technique of flashback,' writes Eliot Weinberger, 'is essentially an artificial rearrangement of chronological sequences; it is not memory-time. The memory thinks simultaneously of beginning, middle, and end; its sense of time is only the loss of time.' Attempting to fit a memory into a linear narrative structure dissolves this complexity. It gives it the wrong shape, producing continuity at the expense of multiplicity. 'Wordsworth and Proust, in their searches for lost time,' Weinberger continues, 'assume that memory is a stream, a stream they follow against its current. But the memory is a vortex, a simultaneity.'

Practising a memory can strengthen your belief in it, even if it's not true. That's how fictions creep in. Hass' grandmother's visits perhaps begin as fantasies, with images and sensations borrowed from other experiences. He plays them over in his mind until, little by little, they become memories, and he believes in them.

These mistakes persist because, as Sacks writes, we have 'no mechanism in the mind or the brain for ensuring the truth...of our recollections', nothing to distinguish true memories from false ones, an unattributed quote from a flash of creation. Or, as Proust has it: 'Facts do not find their way into the world in which our beliefs reside'.

This is as true of Hass' and Sacks' memories as it is of their brothers'. Age and authority are no substitute for proof. In the case of Sacks, the letter supports his brother's version of events, but Hass has no such documentation, so he creates it now. He records his mistake to come to the truth of it, but in the end, it's his brother's word against his. A narrative, after all, provides certainty only of itself. Evidence must come from without. As one of Jorge Luis Borges' narrators says, 'I've told this story so many times I no longer know whether I remember it as it was or whether it's only my words I'm remembering.'

Plato, on the other hand, is suspicious of any knowledge stored outside the mind. He sees writing as a crutch, one that weakens memory. In the *Phaedrus*, he recounts a dialogue in which Socrates calls writing 'an elixir not of memory but of reminding'. He claims writing 'will produce forgetfulness in the souls of those who have learned it, through lack of practice at using their memory, as through reliance on writing they are reminded from outside by alien marks, not from within, themselves by themselves.'

While Plato's faith in the human mind and memory is, in my opinion, misplaced, he's right on one count. How many of us know how and where to find specific information, but retain little of its substance? Perhaps that's why I write this down now, that the truth of things, or at least the narrative of that truth, might be arrived at again, later. That though I won't recall writing this any more than I do copying out *we watched the waves*, I might once more access the feelings that underscore that poem, by returning to this, by going back to 'On Squaw Peak'. We read to remember, write to forget.

How we tell stories about ourselves

It's a road you recognise from a car ad. What's it like to live here
do you think, driving the same winding stretch every night
waiting on set (that is, at home) for your thirty seconds
between snatches of *Law and Order*?

We're already back at the house though, drinking coffee as
morning mist drifts past. We flip a coin to decide who's taking
the kids to soccer and who's going to the beach with our young
loosely clothed friends. They remind me of evangelists, the way they
perform without being prompted, sipping coke, laughing, having a great
time. Later, while you get grass stains out of the whites and I
knock together a no-fuss dinner, all I can think about is fucking them
really going at it. I need to go for a walk

step outside the frame. I think about when we bought our first house
or got our first newspaper subscription (I can't remember which)
and it's apparent, even then, that things are already breaking
down. Projecting forward, we can only wait to see our hearts
breaking, be recast, lose sight of what matters. There were no
simpler times, it turns out, no house by the beach. I don't recognise
anything now, much less go for a drive. But whatever happens
I look forward to looking back on this moment.

Your eyes still move when they're closed

The party moved into the house where we were
bailed up by that photographer. Or maybe he was
a painter—I wasn't really paying attention
horses on my mind.
I remember something about shooting
night for night to capture *eigengrau*
—intrinsic grey—
or painting the pattern behind his eyelids.
Or both.
You can never see nothing, apparently, just as you
can never hear nothing. I refreshed my drink
noticed some scuffing by the stairs.
Hoof marks, maybe. Looking out at the guests
on the lawn, I remembered who he reminded me of
—the photographer, I mean—
but can't remember what reminded me.
We all have our moments of clarity
I guess, visions to be grasped or scuppered
in a blink. Which is fine if you're at a party
but what about when you really want to know?
What does *eigengrau* look like? What
am I not seeing?

The end of things

The future is a fifteen-mile beach on the southern ocean, with its rips and crosscurrents, waves coming in from different directions, collapsing on each other in wash and foam. It's your footsteps being swallowed by a tide that's neither rising nor receding, trying to retrace your tracks to where they leave the waterline, up over the dune, figuring out which path to take through the scrub.

There are signs of others being here—some footprints (not yours), dog tracks, sun-bleached cans and bottles. I pick up some shells, because that's what you do in places like this. I pick out ones that catch my eye: black-striped ones, large ones with flashes of purple and salmon, orange sunbursts. I choose the more distinct shells, but it's a flawed approach. The sand abounds in white and cream-coloured ones shaped like small fans. What I come away with are atypical souvenirs, a non-representative sample.

Either way, I have no desire for shells. Later I'll put them in a box, give them away, discard them. But I'd do the same again, I know I would. We're drawn to these scenes, where everything is salted and breaking down, because it feels like the edge of something. Like the world is reaching up to reclaim things, that it could overwhelm you at any moment. And that's what you want, all there is left to feel. Soon enough, the fading light turns each footstep into mound and shadow, indistinguishable from the other indentations in the sand.

On Zerkalo

after Andrei Tarkovsky

The prevailing sense I'm left with is of wind, not so much in slow motion, but deliberate all the same. It's an early scene: a wide shot of the doctor walking through the field. Nothing moves but his receding figure, until he's about half-way away. He turns back and looks—at us, at the mother by the fence. There's a beat before the wind comes up behind him, rolling out across the grass and rushing the camera. It rattles the trees, gusts again, then stops. The doctor continues on his way.

To me this reflected David Lynch, insofar as what comes after can remind you of what came before. It's about order of exposure—wind in the pines, wind in the fields. There's another scene where Ignat is waiting in his father's apartment. The camera revolves and the boy enters a room where a woman and a servant have appeared. The woman is seated at the table drinking tea, while the maid stands at her side. The woman has Ignat fetch a book and read out a letter by Pushkin. Once he finishes he is told to answer the door: it's his grandmother, but she professes to have the wrong house and promptly leaves. Ignat returns to the room to find the woman and the servant gone too, seemingly vanished. The table has been cleared, but as he approaches it, we see the heat ring, the condensation left by the teapot.

Mountainousness

We came to the mountains
to get away from it all
        driving up after dark
        unloading ourselves onto gravel
but all we found was a crew
clearing the landscape for a set piece.
Their filters brought out the green
and everything was
                        quite suddenly
                    rising peaks and
                                clouding over.
You looked for the sublime
in a box of sultanas. They're not
on the list, but the trees are, the—
        I want to say *cypress*
        but don't know that I'd be right
        or even close
        or that you'd know what I mean.
We can look them up when we get home
after I pick out some good rocks from the
driveway. But we've been through this before
haven't we? I'll put them
in a drawer this time, forget them
or give them away. We knew I would.

Later, on the threshold, we count three things:
        wind
            leaves
                    and a prolonged hesitation between
        sound and sense.
Language slips out and roams the house
like a ghost, careless and clumsy.
The dead mediate the living, it seems
while the lost simply hover out of sight.

We could lie on the floor if we wanted
or sit in separate rooms
        wait for this to pass.
I forgot to look up *cypress*
but it doesn't come up again.
We remember the rocks though
add them to the list.

Inside the bulb

We all occur inside the bulb, waiting to execute our
plans, addiction the only thing to pull us out before the
lights come up. The egg returns because it still seems
honest, even after all these years, cupped in the hand or
left on the table. Today though, today is

a black ceramic bowl, wet leaves like banana skins,
cucumbers that don't mind us so much, the skeleton
in the Japanese restaurant. I take my tablets, avoid
sunlight. You lie down somewhere quiet, hang up thinking

you got in touch too soon. You'll never get to the bottom
of it, but feeling with your toes, locating certain clues,
the important things will sift through. What then?

Ravensburger

We called too soon and got here too early.
No matter, we'll just hang about in the foyer
examine this painting
          of a countryside:
trees and hedges and musketeers
all ready for a masked ball. In the foreground
a girl hands out stage directions, hoping
things will become otherwise (presumably)
but something's either imminent
          or it's not, right? I mean, if I say apple
do you picture it as red or green?
With a worm or a snake or an archer?
Out on the balcony the garden smells like rain
and the forest circumscribes itself
and a horse appears by the brook.
Now might be a good time to peel off
look for more edge pieces. Rain will happen soon
                                        then dusk.

Think, again

Theodor was right. We should put away our pens
pack up the chairs, move inside for a while. In time
all things will pass or be retracted.

Looking out the window
branches, drops bead
poise, come naturally as leaves to be counted
like birds
in system.

The thought of the printing press next to the factory
that burned down, the iron hulk with a beehive
in its bowels.

Here a three-word image
here the coarse black silt.

Twiddle your thumbs
catch your breath in a bottle.
No need to take any of this down really only to
think, again.

Ars memoria

As to memory, I say nobody can equal Simonides!

SIMONIDES OF KEOS

Cast

SKOPAS *of Krannon, nobleman, patron of Simonides*

SIMONIDES *of Keos, his guest, a poet*

KASTOR *and* POLYDEUKES, *the twins*

ALEXANDER LURIA, *neuropsychologist*

S., *his patient, a mnemonist*

FUNES, *the memorious*

YOU *and* I

GRANDMA

Guests and relations of Skopas, doubling as the couple in the auction house

Servant, doubling as auctioneer

[A night to remember]

It happens in Thessaly.
Simonides invited (that is, paid)
to dinner to blow smoke up a host
otherwise endowed:
    Skopas.
Our poet stands
clears his throat. Praises the man
as much as he can before appealing
to Kastor and Polydeukes. An old trick
but a reliable one. He rounds out
                                        with a toast.
For a living, not half bad.

Later, a caller knocks and gives
his name. Stepping onto the porch
Simonides finds nought
                                  but hears
            over his shoulder
            a great creak

                and thunder.

[Blink]

It happens in an instant—

the roof comes down
    crowning the dinner
with stone and pillar
bodies beyond recognition
all but for Simonides
all still but for a servant
moving to raise not the doctor
but the dentist and her records when
                                    Hold the phone
                                    the poet says

        —swifter
than the turning of the long-
                                        winged fly.

[Origin story]

Simonides. Laureate of Athens.
First poet to write for money
turn it to a profession.
Adds four letters to the alphabet
a third note to the lyre.
          Rarely artless
we're told, he measures words with care
    and thought.

Not without critics, though.
    In Aristotle we read of his refusal
to write about the victor
of a mule race. I mean
how could he. But then, how not.
Luckily the winner
    Anaxilas of Rhegium
raised the fee.
                    Hail!
sang Simonides thereafter
transforming the mules
into
                    daughters
                    of storm-footed steeds.

[Look both ways]

In good fortune, posits our poet
each man is noble.
In ill fortune, base.
So which is it to be
for Simonides, standing
on the threshold
of the ruined hall. Why
    we might ask
would the fates spare a poet.

[De oratore]

Why indeed. He knows how this looks
knows what they'll say in the agora.

That the words a certain Simonides
spent on Kastor and his twin
so unimpressed his host.
That Skopas wanted
to hear not the gods and their deeds
reflected, but he and his own.
That because of this he resolved
            in a spirit of

        excessive meanness

to halve the poet's fee.
    After that, they'll say
the poet's words shot red, his silence green
he colluded to taint the cups
contrive a caller
then place the roof square
on the scene.

Watching the replay, we've enough
time to consider whether Skopas
asks for coffee, or just dessert.

What, thinks Simonides
casting an eye upwards
am I gonna tell the cops.

[Knock and run]

Think fast, Simonides
but more so
            think well.

Looking out at fallen stone and timber
at the mangled dead, down at
his barely sullied robes, thinks—
    This smells like Apollo.

Apollo, god of music and poetry and
foremost deity of Keos
from where our poet hails.
                    Not a good look for Simonides.
Better it were the god's father, Zeus
or uncle Poseidon or—come to think of it—
          who was the caller and where did they go.
Did they perceive some tremor
some spine-rending crack that sent them running
before Simonides could answer the door.
Wrong house, most likely

    but they asked for him by name.
Everyone knows you don't just turn up
in a tale like this, leave a guy
standing there
          dick in hand
as the ceiling fissures and falls.

    Unless—

[Heart-devouring sweat]

There is a tale, says Simonides
    turning to face the camera
that virtue dwells on rocks which are hard to climb
and that a company of swift nymphs attends her.
    Pauses. Continues.
Nor may she be seen by the eyes of all mortal men
but only by him in whom heart-
                                        devouring sweat

comes from his marrow
he who comes to the summit by daring.

[Mutatis mutandis]

Simonides knows *what has happened*
cannot be undone but also knows
    more than anyone
that the tale is in the telling
roles can be recast.
So long as the basic outline remains.

    His mind quickens, scans forward
to a time when this has all become myth
when he can calmly review the footage.
    What if, he asks

instead of one
the caller were two. Brothers, perhaps
twins, even. Riding in on horseback
asking for Simonides
    not to draw him out from the banquet
    and save his skin (at least, not only)
but to vanquish Skopas and his kin.
Why—
        for rejecting his praise
        of Kastor and Polydeukes.

Poor Skopas, thinks Simonides.
By denying the twins his home
he admitted them instead
through the roof

into this tale
        cautionary.

[Aetiology]

Simonides turns it over in his mind.
It may well be hard to become a man
                truly noble
and harder still to remain all-blameless.
        But against necessity
    not even the gods fight.

And though the tale comes
not from the horse's mouth
          (our poet shrewd enough
            to know better)
it holds the memory of Skopas
where the record fails. In the end
    he fulfils the commission.
Of course, more useful still
is it to Simonides, serving the poet twice over:
          establishing his wisdom
          while laying out the terms of payment.

    But for now he sees the sky gape
through what was the ceiling
sees the wheel turn
    and a star glint.
He looks again, for the benefit of the camera
and again the star glints
                    not blinking

so much as winking twice.
    Once each
    for Kastor and his twin.

[Analepsis]

Thus it happens
in an instant.

Hold the phone
the poet says.
I remember.

Where once a hall
now only a frame
    and yet
as the servant had served
so would the poet
        preserve
the position of each guest
pictured clearly
    through brick dust
    and rubble.

Their loved ones
he will later walk through the scene
naming the dead.

Here lies Skopas
he'll say

inventing the art of memory

swift as

the turning

of the long-winged fly.

When we talk about the past, we say

I remember.

I remember how it happened.

When we're unsure, we say

I think.

I think that was how.

[A mnemonist]

Cut to the office
of Alexander Luria
two-and-a-half millennia later.

At first he thinks of S. as dull
senseless
a dreamer.
The man doesn't understand why
for instance
he should take down instructions
when he recalls them word for word.
That's how he's come to be here.

Luria teases out his mind by degrees.
He discovers that S. retains things
by converting them
into images
placing them along a street
in his mind. To recall something
he simply goes for a walk.

S. calls his thinking speculative
using the Russian *umozritelny*:
seen with the mind.

[An introduction]

Flash forward another half-century.
This time it's Newcastle
a festival, a gallery busy
with movement and sound
images unfixed, incomplete. Red haze
and cigarettes. You laughing
drinking bad wine
    from a beer bottle.

Who knows what words
we miss
in the din

what's being thought
in that swig between not
                                        knowing
                    and knowing.

We both have other partners
live in other cities.

It's an occasion singular for
the simple fact
                it's when we meet.

[Erratum]

Except it isn't.

There's some other introduction
apparently, some conversation
between panels. Late spring glare
in a corridor in the town hall.
    Have you met.

I can imagine this in a way
that feels like remembering
but it's the party that sticks with me
for no other reason
than having raked it over
            time and again. Looking
for some glimmer
of understanding, perhaps
some sense that a beginning was
                        underway.

Whatever these scenes may be
we've long since talked
these them into a corner

into what we agree
might have happened
and what we can't be sure of.

[Going once]

Let's say this is what I'm thinking about
as we wander through the auction house
its roof ticking in dry April light. The day
takes its pulse
    in an autumn hum
more sound than sense.

The rows determine how the objects
relate to each other, as the auctioneer
calls an occasional table
a chaise longue, a pair of glass ashtrays.

                    Later
once we move from looking at
    to taking home
we'll say we were *buying* a rug.
But for now it feels like browsing
testing wefts and weaves and trying
                    to remember

what we like about our other rug, unable even
to picture its pattern now or name
its colours. Recognition
    it turns out
is different to recollection.
To put it another way
                we'll know it
          when we see it.

[The memorious]

I should say
that S. doesn't stand for
          Simonides

(isn't that a thought)

but that their methods are the same.
Each forms images
for the details to be remembered
sets them against
               a backdrop
as of guests at a dinner.

It's possible, however
that S. is the basis of a Borges
character: Ireneo Funes
a man for whom each word
is marked by a sign

just as S.'s thoughts
and utterances
each have a texture and
each a shape
      to be arranged
as we might furniture.

[Inflections]

At what point did things turn
did Luria realise that S. would retain
every detail of their interactions
in stark
                clarity
while his own memory
would flag and haze over.

He takes notes, sure, but over
the course of thirty years
            of observation
they pale against S.'s recall.

Consider the scene:
    We were in your apartment
says S.
    you at the table and I in the rocking chair
one of their early meetings
    you were wearing a grey suit
    and you looked at me like this.
Like what. The doc flicks through his notes
consults the recording. Like what.
    He doesn't say.

[Cusp]

For that matter, how did you look at me
    in that truncated scene

a year later—a year after
    we met.

If we knew then
what we know now, we could
                                        sit up
    pay attention
pinpoint the moment
when banter became flirting
lust gained purchase
a possible future became
    a likely present.

At the time, though, it felt like any
other night. One that could
just as easily resolve
into nothing as turn a corner.
I waited for a sign
    I remember
while you waited for me
to make a move.
It was three a.m. before
you almost kicked me out.

[A fire]

I want to say
    these moments are important
    only after the fact
but I think I mean
they're important only in the telling

edited for continuity once we know
where things are headed.
    Or, as S. would say
I can only understand
what I can visualise.

More than once
Luria describes him as
                    anchorless
waiting for something
to happen. By his own admission
he's a *Kalter nefesh*
a cold duck.

Say there's a fire
    he says
and I haven't yet begun
to understand what a fire is.

I'd react cold-bloodedly.

[Vessel]

You remember too much
my mother said to me recently.
    This is Anne Carson.
Why hold on to all that?
And I said, Where can I put it down?

The only answer, perhaps, is
    on paper.
But what is too much—too often
        or too many details?

For S., it's the calling up
of images and sensations
that collide with one another.
Say you ask me about a horse.
There's also its colour and taste
to consider, the yard it's penned in—

        which I can't seem
        to get away from myself.

My own mother is
afraid of the opposite
of retaining too little. She's afraid
even before Grandma's diagnosis
            floats to the surface.

[Plateaus]

A silent stroke has no outward symptom
so how do you plot it

as an inflection
or a point along a line.

It starts with a clot in the frontal lobe.
Or the hippocampus
that ancient part of the brain which
negotiates the terms
of memories
from short to long.

Vascular lesions begin to affect
memory and cognition
basic tasks become a challenge.

The decline isn't immediate
nor is it constant.
It's terraced. A sharp plummet

might call you to the nursing home
only to level out
for another four, five, ten years.

Until the next drop comes.

[Kindness]

What if forgetfulness were not
a flaw
but the other side of the coin.
A way to stop a surge of detail from bursting
the banks
while its twin, memory, lets us
make sense of the world.

I suspect he was not very capable of thought
says Borges' narrator.
To think is to forget differences
generalise

make abstractions.

In order to get to sleep
Funes would turn his mind
from the world

imagine himself
at the bottom of the river
annihilated by the current.

When we talk about imagining things
we talk about thinking.

I was thinking about.

[A cold duck]

Luria describes what he writes of S.
as an unimagined portrait
confident he knows where observation
                                        leaves off
and invention begins.

S. imagines in a way that feels
like seeing. He speculates.

    To me
there's no great difference
between the things I imagine
and what exists in reality.

He can look at a clock
and see the hands remain
in place
unmoving
    for hours at a time.

That's why I'm often late.

[Anagnorisis]

The first time I visit her
in the nursing home
She doesn't know who I am.
Reaches for a name.

I wish, in this moment
I'd kept in closer contact.
Just as later I'll wish I'd visited more.
But then I picture myself fumbling
through a phone call with a person
I've ceased to know
    who doesn't understand
who they're talking to
in that grey area between
        recognition
    and recollection.

The horse has already bolted.
She's already drinking
            from that river.

[That's nice]

Her go-to phrase.
It's what she says
    on her birthday
emaciated and bent
skin papery as we goad her
through the occasion.
    That's nice.

I'm glad to take part
to have a half-conversation
unsure if she thinks me

a grandson
or simply a visitor.
I'm glad when it's over.

When I start to get sick, S. remarks
I imagine the illness is passing.
I know it doesn't work like this but

            sometimes
I think I can cure myself
if I imagine it clearly enough.

[Thinking into]

She goes not much later.
I don't recall when
just that it comes with relief

marking a subtle change
rather than a distinct moment

part of a broader shift
that takes place
over weeks, months
          years.

The nursing home stays with me.
We could go back now
if we wanted. Anyone
can walk in

but only those
who understand
how the code by the door
relates to the keypad
   can leave

find somewhere to put things down.

[Imāgō]

People once thought seahorses
grew into hippocamps

those storm-footed steeds
that pull Poseidon's chariot.
Just as *image* and *imagination*
share the same root
    —imāgō—
both creatures have
the head of a horse
and the tail of a fish.

Which is exactly what the god of the sea
needs to broach tide and shore
waves and quakes reducing
to memory
            all in his wake.

When I hear the word nothing
    says S.
I see a cloud, thin
and transparent. And when
I try to seize a particle of this nothing
    I get the most minute particle.

[Dorian mode]

If an *imago*
is the ideal image you carry of someone
    from childhood

what's the other side of that

the image you have of someone
in the present, that you use
to edit the past.

A couple wanders through the furniture
trying to align their taste, objects
arranged like images
set against a backdrop
    bristling with facts and details
waiting to be released.

The warehouse swells.

When I think of how you looked
when we first met

it's exactly
as you appear to me now.

[Ars oblīvium]

Forgetting doesn't feel
like anything
    remember.
It's trying to recall
that has a texture
rooting about in what feels familiar
        but escapes you still.

Writing something down
means I know I won't have to remember it
    says S.
But it doesn't work. Neither does burning
the pieces of paper. He discovers
                eventually
that only when he doesn't want
to remember something
        he can finally stop seeing it.

When the cameras stop rolling
Simonides offers
to teach his method to
Themistocles. The leader of Greece
is unconvinced. He replies
    to wit

You'd be doing me a greater kindness
if you taught me to forget
what I wanted
than if you taught me to remember.

False nostalgia

Monte Tabor is a hill in Recanati, on the east coast of Italy. It's a hundred-odd metres from the house where, in the early nineteenth century, Giacomo Leopardi wrote many of the lyrics and canzoni that make up his *Canti*, his life's great work. On the side of the hill you can find, carved in stone, the phrase '*Sempre caro mi fu quest'ermo colle*'—'This lonely hill was always dear to me'. It's the opening line from his idyll, '*L'infinito*' ('Infinity'), in which, despite the hedgerow blocking his view, he sees with his mind 'unending spaces, / and superhuman silences, and depthless calm'.

In another poem, '*Alla luna*' ('To the moon'), Leopardi describes himself climbing the same hill. He gazes at the moon and reminisces about doing just that as a young man:

> And yet it helps me, thinking back, reliving
> the time of my unhappiness.
> Oh in youth, when hope has a long road ahead
> and the way of memory is short,
> how sweet it is remembering what happened,
> though it was sad, and though the pain endures!

When Leopardi casts his youth as the specific time of unhappiness, it's important to note, firstly, that he's only twenty-one when he writes this. Secondly, he's no more content as an adult. Indeed, it's hard to find a writer more committed to his own unhappiness—he's the poet to whom Nietzsche and Schopenhauer look for inspiration. He's already published the work that will define him as Italy's foremost modern poet, '*All'Italia*' ('To Italy'), but this does little to alleviate his torment. His health is shot and the melancholia that defined his adolescence continues unabated. The pain endures.

And yet it helps him. The poem is steeped in sorrow but is not, in the end, regretful. Crying before the moon is a source of pleasure for Leopardi, a reverie. He looks back fondly on times that were sad, savours his tears.

The history of nostalgia starts with a diagnosis, a 'sad mood originating from the desire to return to one's native land'. The condition is first described, in 1688, by Johannes Hofer, a Swiss doctor treating mercenaries for symptoms of nausea, fever, loss of appetite, voices in the head, heart attack and suicide. Hofer combines the Greek words νόστος (*nóstos*, homecoming) and ἄλγος (*álgos*, pain) to give his homesickness a name. His patients have the tendency to lose touch with the present, to confuse it with the past, to conflate real and imaginary events.

By Leopardi's time, nostalgia has moved away from being an affliction and has become a poetic trope, a sentimental longing for a time or place or set of conditions that has been lost. It becomes a commonplace not just of Romantic work but also of civil poetry, an Italian verse form inspired by the high rhetoric of the ancient Greeks, drawing a line through Dante and Petrarch and on to later exponents like Pier Paolo Pasolini. In Leopardi's civil poetry, his canzoni, nostalgia consists of public lamentation, a yearning for earlier eras. Poems like '*All'Italia*' excoriate his country's present condition and appeal to her ancient glory. Italy in the 1820s is divided, with Recanati occupied by Napoleon, her sons conscripted to conflicts abroad—'making war / in foreign lands'—that is, in the same conditions that led Hofer to invent nostalgia in the first place. Leopardi desires, in this poem, for more worthy struggles to write about, imagining what Simonides of Keos might have said at the battle of Thermopylae, 'climbing the Antela hill' to survey 'the sky and shore and land' where his countrymen had died:

> The stars will fall from the sky and into the sea
> and scream as they're put out
> before we forget you
> and our love for you will die.

In Leopardi's lyric poetry, nostalgia takes a different form. His reflection in '*Alla luna*' is sentimental and nostalgic, but the conditions of the past are hardly lost to him. He's barely an adult, standing on the same hill as he had in youth, gazing at the same moon and with the same sadness. The only difference between his present and his past, the only irretrievable aspect, is time, which is neither the cause of his lament nor its object; indeed, it barely gets a look in. The past doesn't want for reinstatement here, only its evocation. For Leopardi, indulging the memory is enough.

And so we discover a different kind of nostalgia, one that looks back wistfully on moments that weren't happy, on times that weren't stable, on events that weren't enjoyable. It's that time you missed the last train and waited on the station all night, bored and cold and running out of cigarettes. It's that house you lived in where the unsealed walls shed brick dust in the night while the neighbours dealt drugs. It doesn't fit the common definition of nostalgia but it's not strictly false, either. It reflects a genuine fondness for previous events and periods in your life, despite their flaws. How sweet it is remembering what happened, though it was sad, and though the pain endures.

Georges and Anne Laurent are hosting a dinner party. The film is Michael Haneke's *Caché*, the characters played by Daniel Auteuil and Juliette Binoche respectively. The doorbell rings. Georges gets up to answer it, opens the front door, then the metal gate, out onto the quiet Paris street. No one there.

While Georges is outside, the roof doesn't collapse on the guests. When he comes back in, however, something blocks the door. It's a videotape—an old VHS—wrapped in a drawing of a rooster bleeding from the neck. It's been placed there, seemingly by magic, in the brief moment he was outside.

The sequence is unnerving, not because of the drawing, and not because someone couldn't have snuck in behind Georges, or couldn't have been hiding inside the gate—between it and the front door—waiting to deposit the package before creeping out again (*caché* translates as *hidden*). Nor is it because Georges doesn't see them do it. No, the reason it doesn't sit right is because *we* don't see the phantom mailman. Our point of view in this scene moves between a position a few feet behind Georges, on the porch, and Georges' perspective, as he looks up and down the street. We are effectively standing in the doorway when the package is left there. It defies physics, breaks the rules.

When Georges returns to the party, they watch the tape. It's a video shot from inside a car in the rain. It shows a house in the country: the house where Georges grew up. We don't know who's behind the camera.

Caché opens with an uninterrupted shot of the outside of Georges and Anne's house. It's taken from across the street, a short distance up a laneway. Someone walks past, Anne leaves for work. Nothing is happening, the kind of nothing that predicates violence. The scene runs longer than is comfortable. We wait for a trauma to split the moment into before and after.

When it comes, the split is gentle, anticlimactic. We simply hear Georges and Anne's voices over the top of the visual before they fast-forward the tape on which the scene is playing. It turns out what we've been watching for the last few minutes is not (at least, not only) from our perspective, but from that of an unseen character, a stalker. This stalker is presumably the person who delivers the tape during the dinner party, and later another tape, one that guides Georges to the door of a flat in one of the outer arrondissements.

The flat belongs to Majid, an Algerian man whom Georges, as a child, dissuaded his parents from adopting. Majid's parents worked for the Laurents. They were murdered, along with 200 others, in the police massacre of October 1961, a reprisal against the Algerian independence movement. Majid subsequently grew up in an orphanage, while Georges remained in the house shown in the dinner-party tape. The resulting difference between Majid's and Georges' lives is distinct. Georges sees the tapes as an attempt at revenge. Majid denies them.

A different kind of nothing takes place in the final shot of the film, a nothing that could be something. A character approaches the Laurents' son, Pierrot, on the steps of his school. We can't hear what they're saying, but Pierrot seems trusting, if a little apprehensive. Have they met before? The man appears friendly, but he's much taller and older than Pierrot. After a few moments, he leaves. Pierrot returns to his friends, and soon they leave as well. The camera stays where it is, watching schoolchildren mill about on the steps. Is the scene shot by Haneke, for us, the audience, or is it like the opening sequence, a tape shot by the stalker? The intervening film is the attempt to discover this hidden antagonist.

My first impression of *Caché* is not good. The long stationary shots feel indulgent, intended to make us uncomfortable for the sake of doing so. Haneke seems to delight in setting up thriller conventions just to spurn them, leave them unresolved. A suspected kidnapping of Pierrot turns out to be a miscommunicated sleepover. The tapes, the anonymous phone calls, the creepy drawings—these are all implicit threats, not resulting in a climax or redemption, but simply in Georges' anger and threats of his own.

The main characters range from flawed to frustrating: Georges is a liar, Anne unfaithful, and Pierrot, for his part, a brat. They lead a privileged middle-class existence with which we can identify but not sympathise. The stalker's message to them is clear enough: *You're being watched*. But what does that mean? What is it they should fear? The primary suspect, Majid, is gentle, sentimental, resigned. Haneke builds the expectation of violence over the course of the film, but when the moment arrives, it is quick, unexpected and uncomfortable, with Majid killing himself.

After this, Majid's son confronts Georges at his office, but this too yields no epiphany. The son denies being behind the tapes, Georges admits no guilt. Georges doesn't waste any time examining his conscience either, taking the afternoon off and going home for a nap.

In the final scene, the man who approaches Pierrot appears to be Majid's son. What does he say? What *could* he say? Do they know each other? We have no way of decoding this scene, no way of understanding what's going on or what might happen next. What does any of it mean?

The film ends without revealing who sent the tapes, or why, unresolved at both a plot and an emotional level.

I find the inscrutability unsatisfying. I say as much to my girlfriend. We talk about it in the pub afterward, taking more enjoyment from the conversation than from the film.

And yet.

The film stays with me, sits at the back of my mind. I find myself asking questions like: *What does it mean to watch?*

When we first see Georges and Anne, we see them through the eyes of the stalker. We join him in his watching (we presume it's a *him*; so do the characters), but we also join Georges and Anne, watching themselves being watched. This doubling is further complicated by scenes that are filmed twice, such as when Georges confronts Majid in his flat. Initially we see the scene through Haneke's camera, then through the voyeur's camera (technically also Haneke's camera, but the distinction remains), which has been planted in the flat to capture the interaction. On a number of occasions, Haneke shoots from a perspective first introduced to us by the stalker, including that of the opening scene, across the street from the Laurents' house. The effect of these interlaced perspectives is that we're never completely sure who's filming, what we're seeing, who else is watching.

So when it comes to the final scene, a stationary, unedited long shot from middle distance—similar to one from earlier in the film—we ask whether we're viewing it from our perspective, as audience, or if we're gatecrashing the stalker's private show. Has Majid's son set up a hidden camera to stage the scene? That would mean Majid, now dead, was innocent all along. It would also mean that the Laurents' saga will continue.

But Haneke withholds the information we require to be certain of anything in this scene, and in doing so, creates several layers of irresolution. The stalking might be over, it might not. The scene could be another tape, but this doesn't mean Majid's son is filming it. Majid's son may be the man in front of the camera, talking to Pierrot, but we can't be sure. And if the scene is not a tape, this neither confirms Majid as the stalker, nor does it exonerate him. The very unresolvedness of the narrative is uncertain.

All this keeps my thoughts coming back to the film. Without seeing it again, my opinion shifts. Within a fortnight, I'm recommending it. Now, I count it among my favourites.

Caché is not about nostalgia. It's about guilt and responsibility and collective memory. It's about the trauma arising out of a specific period in France and what it did to Algerians in the name of keeping the peace. It's not just that the film is unresolved, but that the whole mess of French colonialism, of relations with Algeria, of cultural amnesia, has no resolution.

The drawings—those which come with the tapes—are from Georges and Majid's shared memory. They depict the lies Georges told to get Majid sent to the orphanage: that Majid is coughing blood, that Majid kills a rooster to scare him. When shown one of the drawings, Majid recognises it, but denies responsibility. If he didn't draw it, where did it come from? Georges' id? Or is it the work of Majid's son, the caretaker of memory in the next generation?

Georges feels no remorse for his actions as a child. He's unable to acknowledge his role in changing the course of Majid's life. Confronted with the consequences of his past actions, the only thing he can think to do is apologise.

ANNE
You say *sorry* and just like that
everything's okay, right?

GEORGES
Am I supposed to beg? What did
I do that's so awful?

But what can an apology accomplish, when the system of privilege and oppression which orphaned Majid is still in place, when Georges' position in that system remains unchallenged? When the Laurents think Pierrot has been kidnapped by the stalker, Georges leads the police to Majid's apartment. They enter it with violence, without a warrant, arrest Majid and his son and keep them overnight on suspicion, without charge. Pierrot, meanwhile, is at a friend's house. He doesn't call because he's punishing his mother—he found out she's having an affair.

When Majid kills himself, Georges doesn't call an ambulance. He goes to see a movie. When Anne asks if he should tell the police, his first thought is that Majid wants him to be a suspect in his death. Our first thought: *Was he being filmed?*

As an audience, we expect narratives to follow certain rules, which is why we feel cheated when the tape is left in the door without our seeing it—it breaks the contract that's been established between us and the director. Haneke asks us to consider how these expectations implicate us in the events of the film, in what happens to the characters. What are the ethics of watching? Are we any less guilty than the stalker? In what ways are we responsible for what happens to the Laurents, for what happens to Majid?

Throughout *Caché* our perspective is constantly linked to the actions of the voyeur. We see what they see, looking in on the Laurents' world. The final scene could be shot by Haneke, as director, and not by the stalker, but does that make that much of a difference?

Throughout the *Canti*, Leopardi invites his readers to consider the difference between pleasure and happiness. For him, happiness is a condition not just denied to melancholics like himself, but to everyone. In the canzoni, happiness exists primarily as a thing of the past, and the closest he can get to it, from the sorry state of present-day Italy, is to honour the courage of the ancients and exhort his compatriots to restore their country to her former greatness.

This might lead us to think Leopardi believes happiness *can* be achieved, if only certain changes in the nation's fortunes would come to pass. Not so. '[L]ife produces nothing, / only senseless suffering', he writes in '*Le ricordanze*' ('The recollections'). Unhappiness is, for him, the human condition, its natural state. It's also exactly what makes life bearable, especially when you consider the alternatives. In his journal of ideas, impressions and philosophical observations, the *Zibaldone*, he writes: 'Despair is much, but much more pleasurable than boredom.'

Pleasure, for Leopardi, is something that can be achieved despite unhappiness, even because of it. 'Oh happy one for whom lament was life!' he writes in '*Ad Angelo Mai*' ('To Angelo Mai'). In '*Nella nozze della sorella Paolina*' ('On the marriage of his sister Paolina'), he says, after advising his sister to raise unhappy children rather than cowardly ones:

> The man whose soul cannot take pleasure
> when the winds rage and the sky
> fills with clouds and thunder strikes
> the hills, has not known love.

It's this approach that so interests Nietzsche and Schopenhauer, and leads Italo Calvino to label him an 'unhappy hedonist'. Leopardi doesn't mourn the loss of youth or his illusions so much as he takes an elegiac pleasure in the impossibility of their return. 'Hopes, hopes: O bright illusions / of my early years!' he writes in '*Le ricordanze*'. Looking back on his youth, he sees no simpler times, just more optimistic ones, when hope has a long road ahead. The only difference, between then and now, is that the road no longer exists.

My change of heart with *Caché* is interesting to me, not because I failed to enjoy something that might very well be unenjoyable (an argument often made about Haneke's films), but that I failed to value the experience. The resulting shift is significant, not in my appreciation of the film as a film, as a *potential* experience, but in my *actual* experience, that of sitting in a cinema and seeing that film at that time.

This is a kind of remembrance that locates meaning in an experience in spite of its unenjoyability, transforming instances that were of little worth in the past into ones that are productive in the present. There's no redemption here, no lesson learnt, just an attitudinal change. The core, inscribed details of watching *Caché* remain the same, but how I consider the event now, how I look back fondly on a negative experience, that's what intrigues me.

In Leopardi's approach to memory-making we see the natural extension of this type of remembrance, its counterpoint. He retraces his steps up Monte Tabor, looks to the moon and thinks: *Remember this.*

The episode is staged twice over. He recreates it, first in real life, to connect with his past self, to evoke the feelings of his youth. At the same time he puts it down in verse, to relive it again later. In this way, the event recorded in the poem isn't just one of remembrance, but the conscious creation of a memory. He's driven by a desire to preserve the experience, just as Marcel seeks to capture the sensation brought on by the madeleine. Proust writes: 'I want at least to be able to ask of it again and find again, intact, available to me, soon, for a decisive clarification.'

This type of nostalgia, then, isn't just about locating value in flawed experiences. It's about actively creating them. It's finding yourself alone, looking out at the southern ocean, projecting forward and asking yourself, as Leopardi does in '*Il passero solitario*' ('The solitary thrush'):

> How shall I see these years? And how they're spent?
> I know I shall repent,
> And often, uncomforted, I shall look back.

Leopardi, as you can imagine, is often facing the past. It is knowledge of the present, he says in 'Le ricordanze', that replaces the sweetness of memory:

> with pain, and a vain desire

for the past, however sad, and the wish
to say: I was.

In the *Zibaldone* he writes that 'the present, whatever it may be, cannot be poetic; and the poetic, in one way or another, always consists in the distant, the indefinite, the vague.' As Calvino points out, Italian is the only language in which the word *vago* (vague) also means 'lovely, attractive'.

Reflecting on an experience as it happens anticipates a future outside your current emotional state. It's *one day you'll look back on this and laugh*. You construct the story as it occurs, watch yourself living into the narrative.

It's the same thing we do when we take a photograph: creating the moment through posing, interrupting an instant to capture it. It's easy to imagine Leopardi taking shot after failed shot of himself up on that hill, unable to get the white balance right with the ambient light of the moon, trying to imbue the photos with 'some remains of my past feelings, placed there so it might be kept and last through time, as though in store'.

But it's the early nineteenth century, so he's not taking photos but writing verses, hoping that, later in life, 'they will warm my old age with the heat of my youth'. He looks forward to looking back. He wants 'to reflect on who I was, and to compare myself with myself'.

Elsewhere in the *Zibaldone* he writes that 'almost all pleasures of the imagination and feeling consist of remembering'. In '*Le ricordanze*' he claims: 'There's nothing here I see or feel / but that some image doesn't live in me again'. Once more we can find a similar attitude in Proust, for whom each new experience is completed only in recollection. Because 'reality takes shape only in memory', Marcel says, 'the flowers I am shown today for the first time do not seem to me to be real flowers.' To reach their fullness, they must be inscribed in memory and revisited there.

For Leopardi, this is 'Over and above the remembering', a way to reconstitute the past, to ensure its continuation and, therefore, the continuation of his self. The pain endures.

There's little to be gained by debating whether photos reproduce reality any better than Leopardi's verses do, whether posing creates an artificial moment, whether these moments are more representative than natural ones. Quite simply, photos capture people in the act of being in a photo, nothing more.

In *Caché*, we watch characters watching themselves. Georges is equal parts shaken and nonplussed by the tapes because he lives his life in images. He's the host and producer of a television show, more than comfortable seeing himself reflected on the screen. We view him on set and in the editing suite, controlling his image and the images made of him. Throughout their ordeal, the Laurents regularly step outside the present moment to watch their past or edit their future.

Watching yourself in the moment might remove you from the moment, but it's also become integral to *being in the moment*. You participate in the here and now by processing events as they happen and considering how you might reflect on them later. And then, later, you step out of another moment to look back on and form a genuine connection with this one.

This makes the passing of time meaningful, providing a set of behaviours that relieve you of the burden—or banality—of the raw experience. This isn't a false way of living, just a narrativised one. If we're not consuming the story of ourselves, we're actively generating and recording it. Images create the moment they capture. These moments construct our autobiographies. They provide both inspiration and evidence for the stories we tell about ourselves. We engage by disengaging.

In Don DeLillo's *White Noise*, the narrator, Jack, and his academic offsider, Murray, take a trip to see the most photographed barn in America. When they get there they don't see the barn so much as the hundreds of people 'taking pictures of taking pictures'. '"No one sees the barn,"' says Murray:

> "We see only what the others see. The thousands who were here in the past, those who will come in the future. We've agreed to be part of a collective perception."

The fear of missing out has been surpassed by the fear of going unrecorded, of not documenting our experience. We try to watch the waves so that later we can say *we watched the waves*.

Again, Murray:

> "What was the barn like before it was photographed?" he said. "What did it look like, how was it different from other barns, how was it similar to other barns? We can't answer these questions because we've read the signs, seen the people snapping the pictures. We can't get outside the aura. We're part of the aura. We're here, we're now."

We climb Monte Tabor not to look at the moon but to include it in a poem. Or an essay. What was it like before Leopardi got here? There's no way to know, no escaping the aura. So we stage our own memories, photograph the inscription—*Sempre caro mi fu quest'ermo colle*—the image serving as its own caption, its rationale, its explanation. Because ultimately it helps us, looking back, this nostalgia that's over and above remembering.

Immediately before Majid kills himself, he says to Georges, 'I wanted you to be present.'

Autoplagiarism

Ungainly

Let's set the scene: me, back at the beach, unsure
if I'm on time or much too late. There's a lot
gone unsaid, but that's not really the problem.
It's more that I don't want to keep explaining myself

not while water laps at my heels, roiling, ungainly
ready to pull a person under. That's the menace, see.
That, and not being able to escape the feeling
that an allosaurus might, at any moment, bound

over the dune and seize that plesiosaur from the water.
They'll thrash away until one or the other dies
or escapes or gives up, as it is with most things.
Still, I'd rather idle here, unable to come

to the phone, thinking on all the plans
we'll never see through, menu options
and then, unexpectedly, the weather. Nothing
to indicate the shift afoot. No, that will occur

by miniscule changes until you see
nought but red, until it vibrates and makes
you sick and movement occurs as if through
a liquid. You won't notice until your life

doesn't recognise you. That's when you might
find yourself standing on a beach with a pocket
full of shells, thinking, *ungainly* is the word
yes, and that sometimes

things merely happen the way they do.

Purge Landscape (the wolf in the fairytale)

This is where the fog came through the trees
and left behind a unified scene[1]. A path
leads up the hill, the vanishing point
over your shoulder. Near the treeline
                                        the cabin.

There's a key under the mat, he said. I can't remember
his face, but then, neither can you. You'd rather
a room with a sideboard, a desk, a mantle. Take
a seat and a quill
see what the three of you can achieve.

To be able
    to turn to writing
to lay down on the page, to lie in lieu of words, letters, script—

turning with thought, yes, but without force
as I might to a newspaper or a stand of birch.
If you tilt your head
    just right
you can hear the walls' whispered sanctions. Outside
swallows skirt the ground, a felled tree

---

[1] a landscape a clearing a toilet block this is where he approached us me and glenn a wolf in drag a sheep in daywear *lupus in fabula* granny-fabulous and all what's-the-time-mister but we were just minding our

opens up perspective. Seeing is
what we know it is
            but for the gradual process beneath all things.

                        Saucepan milk
and the scrape of the chair leg. There's a knock at the
door and we don't know which way to look. If we're
            perfectly still
they'll go away, go and bother the neighbours
or something. We can hide in the cupboard if we need to
wait for this all to blow over.

What does the past disclose about itself?
There's a figure up on the hill, a blur at first
brought on by wind, brought closer by it.
    It loiters, pauses, poised, looks back
despite the darkness it looks

while behind the scene an ibis rises
over the synoptic chart, disappears into the canopy.
The storm arrives and the cold arrives and the rain strikes
sound from the roof. And so here we are

---

business officer i swear not really my type anyway not ready to lose my dignity down a rabbit hole not if he makes me wear a red raincoat but

you and I. Things shift
and we become inflected. After the rain
three fires start
    and glimmer

if only for a moment
—a lantern, a campfire, an unknown quantity—
broken by long intervals

here, then here, then here.

It's nothing, you'll say in the morning. *Something got into
the garden, that's all*. Knocked pots, chewed leaves
traces in the dust. I see my reflection slicing bread while you
straighten the picture on the wall
    hills and meadows
    a still oak against clouds and watercolour.

What is it that you want? I ask, gently kicking the sideboard
all the while thinking *crows* and *light green*. We know
the wind by the smoke from the boiler stove
    the line of ash on the floor
        driven by an unseen hand
                circling motes

---

my what a big mouth he had all the better for telling stories i guess for quoting heidegger you only have to reach under so many bushes to to be caught in the corner of your eye.

Oh, I don't know, you say, *we could go for a drive, perhaps listen to speech break down on the radio.*

It takes but one slip
the tip of my index finger
clean at the knuckle

bone, skin, nail
and the pad of flesh on the underside.

It lands with a small thud.
We dig a hole behind the cabin
and return it to its roots.

Is it conviction that holds things together or just a gentle acceptance? On the mantelpiece, the lamp with the moth-eaten shade

a small china cup, a photo of me in more certain times when we could be sure of who was counting the leaves and the names of people we knew. I'm sitting on a log before a grove of trees

---

find lupine sympathies round here to find someone hoping to grasp the thingness of the thing but not me officer i left glenn to it thought he'd be

and off behind
in the bushes
two shapes, not quite in focus.
You straighten the picture again

(this one or the clouds one, it doesn't matter)

and I think, *is anyone behind that tree?*
When the bleeding stops, we should stretch our legs
in the woods. But we won't
not yet.
We'll wait amid this torpor worn thin
and thinner
reduced and reserved
off to one side.

---

fine *tocca ferro* last thing i saw was him looking into that mouth peering down that throat *in bocca al lupo* is he alright do you know

A note on 'Purge Landscape'

I left out the painter we paid
to show us what it would've been like
if we'd built our house over there
if it would've given us a clearer picture of things.
He's the one behind the tree. Also, I left out your
sighing, your picking pieces of bark off the trunk.
And the part where the path becomes
a metaphor. That behind us
one thing follows another.

a conversation between carriages

i can smell your coming after me your running down
the platform your footfalls muffled by shunting carriages
but i knew you'd be late you always are which is why i'm
laughing like the little train that could steaming away
through the suburbs through the hinterland to where
the next scene takes place me tied to the track showing
off my caboose one last time one last fight atop the
sleeper car except there won't be a tussle today not until
you learn to be punctual to orient yourself to express
your feelings

we pass the port round the bay enter a tunnel and
shortly i'll be gone and missing you no doubt but gone
all the same at least until the train starts slowing comes
to a stop delayed for some reason lights flickering
then failing for some reason and everything becomes
crystal clear don't ask me how but somehow i know
you've sailed east from the dateline into yesterday into
nowadays tossing your reputation overboard and i know
that when we start moving again when we emerge from
this gloom you'll be in the dining car the light violet
you calm under pressure me a little anxious but again
i'll be on time maybe even early i'll be waiting i'll be
prepared which is why i'm laughing again because you'll
miss your chance again let time leave you behind i mean
we both knew it was over right this is all i'm saying all

that's going through my head as i catch that scent that
unmistakable scent wafting in from the vestibule

this doesn't mean we're back together

Rangoli
or: Zeno in the suburbs

just as we require an unbroken line
with no gaps where evil spirits may enter
you should never set foot in a supermarket
without a strategy, knowing
    as you do
that you'll emerge hours later
with impulses and objects
refusing to cohere into a meal
the shuffle and hum before the auto-doors
before turning yourself out
to face the bridge and tunnel crowd
who never lose the day or their place in it
milling in the carpark
any excuse to come close enough to stroke your elbow
groaning through the static
the secret of the continuous line
                            the dot.

Out of politeness

Out of politeness you probably wouldn't say
especially when spring has started false
and hailstones
small as ball bearings
ring the roof
keeping you trapped at the library
a cancelled anatomy book under your arm
—or perhaps it's a newspaper
and instead you're under the eaves
looking out at leaf eddies.

If asked, I probably wouldn't say, either
instead imagining myself beside an orchard
surrounded by the heady aroma
    of peaches
enjoying this lapse into drizzle
fingers deep in the soil.

Would you say *nothing*, though
if asked
if pressed between pages
if, while hours and minutes trickled by
if I
if—
I probably wouldn't say *no*
no, not when time's fragments gather together
in a room like boxes on a calendar grid.

I wouldn't want to say *either*, either
or *as well.*
I wouldn't want to say anything, no
not nothing, not no, not probably not
lips stitched against the apologia
of a coming wind
needling, addressing no one
and giving everything away.

Associative Disorder

That's no proper way to hold a cat, she says, pork fingers splayed
across its chest. A rustle of wet leaves. Wet leaves don't rustle, they–

Look, again. It moved. Knows we're watching. I thought
it was me, but it's just someone dressed like me. A life measured

in handspans. Somehow a clumsy word like *goodness* makes
its way in. Meet me by the phone in the foyer, coax a non-event

into being, brush your pants on wet grass. From the doorway:
how to suggest a colour without naming it? More importantly

how to be less liminal. Is the cat even hungry? Yes
and no.

Geese

Pay no attention to those geese
that remind you of your aunt

  they have the same fat ankles
  only it's their necks that are fat
  but then, they don't
  have fat necks at all
  so what is it about them?

Let's take another turn
about the pond, see if we can't
remember the last time
we had an experience.

A little about me

Climbing out the window, down the drainpipe, already I feel more sincere. The path curls out from the walled garden, white flowers growing in clumps, replicas up in the greenhouse. He takes the postcard: *This is where you're from?* The image is pixelated. A hedge maze wants for a straight line. Is this a productive relationship? I tell him it's all about self.

Everything all the time

Isn't this what you wanted?
A not-quiteness
an almost-realness
someone to interpret the unknown?
There's a difference between open-ended
and non-committal
                                        and I thought
knowing this would get us across the line.
Failure implies the possibility of success
                                                    I guess

but it's not enough
to just see how things turn out—not always.
What do you do all day, anyway?
You have that job of yours
but where is it going?
The trick is understanding when to move fast
                                                    be dismissive
or just do
        one thing.
It's about plans and timelines.
If you could water the plants while I'm away
        that might work. I mean
then we'd know what books to read
                                    and songs to sing
                                    and shoes to wear.

The garbage goes out on Wednesday
this window doesn't lock.

The problem is less
that we can't get there

it's that we think we can.

Regression to the mean

A jar, a thought, a slight breeze. Who else is tired of these props
and found objects? Left on their own
they form connections, attach to each other, signal new meanings.
And while we wait in the wings for the next act to begin
for a guiding principle to wander by
we might as well reset the scene:
the one in the cabin in the forest, perhaps, or
the one by the water, that epitomised landscape—
the sand, the beach house, the predictable sets.

Thinking on it now, it should never have been about
what was missing from that moment
        just about being there. But you can't identify a problem
you're in the middle of, and we can't go back
and do it over, even when the map is spread before us
tracing paths up through the hills. Best not to think of yourself
as the driving force, as the protagonist of your life
but more as an empty vessel
or a thought on the wind.

No matter what the subject, the memory always thinks of something else, is always creating still lifes, collages. The pure (impossible) biography or autobiography would create constellations out of one mind's associations, distractions, incongruous leaps; it would be regardless of time.

ELIOT WEINBERGER

Notes

Page *vii* Drake: 'Unforgettable', *Thank Me Later*, 2010

Page *vii* Perec: *Life a user's manual*, trans. David Bellos, Collins Harvill, London, 1988

'Anamnesis'

Page 6 'everything set in…others': Bruce Beaver, 'Earth and Fern-Softened Rock-Face', *Anima and Other Poems*, UQP, St Lucia, 1994

'A note on We Watched the Waves'

Page 24 'Still later, on…law.': Robert Hass, *Human Wishes*, The Ecco Press, New York, 1989

Page 24 'My brother, four…air.': Hass, *Time and Materials*, Ecco, New York, 2007

Page 25 'You never saw…there.': Oliver Sacks, 'Speak, Memory', *The New York Review of Books*, February 21, 2013

Page 26 'We have each…narrations.': Sacks, *The Man Who Mistook His Wife for a Hat*, Picador, London, 1986

Page 27 'A person's life…architecture.': Italo Calvino, *Mr Palomar*, trans. William Weaver, Secker & Warburg, London, 1985

Page 28 'The Western technique…a simultaneity.': Eliot Weinberger, 'Matteo Ricci', *Works on Paper*, New Directions, New York, 1986

Page 29 'no mechanism in...recollections': Sacks, 'Speak, Memory'

Page 29 'Facts do not...reside': Marcel Proust, *The Way by Swann's*, trans. Lydia Davis, Penguin, Camberwell, 2002

Page 29 'I've told this...remembering.': Jorge Luis Borges, 'The Night of the Gifts', *The Book of Sand*, trans. Norman Thomas di Giovanni, Allen Lane, London, 1979

Page 30 'an elixir not...themselves by themselves.': Plato, *Phaedrus*, trans. Christopher Rowe, Penguin, London, 2005

'Ars memoria'

This sequence is indebted first and foremost to Anne Carson's work—specifically *Economy of the Unlost*—and formally and stylistically to Christopher Logue's *War Music* and Paul Muldoon's *Madoc: a mystery*.

Page 41 'As to memory...Simonides!': Quoted by Aristides in *Orationes* [28.59], via Anne Carson, *Economy of the Unlost*, Princeton University Press, New Jersey, 1999

Page 45 'Rarely artless': Carson, *Economy of the Unlost*

Page 45 'Hail, daughters of...steeds!': Aristotle, quoted in and translated by C.M. Bowra, *Greek Lyric Poetry: From Alcman to Simonides*, Oxford University Press, London, 1936

Page 46 'excessive meanness': Cicero, *De oratore*,

trans. E.W. Sutton, Harvard University Press, Cambridge, Mass., 1976

Page 49 'There is a tale…daring': *Greek Lyric Poetry*

Page 49 'what has happened…undone': *Greek Lyric Poetry*

Page 55 'dull / senseless / a dreamer': Quotes and paraphrases of S. and Luria are from A.R. Luria, *The Mind of a Mnemonist*, trans. Lynn Solotaroff, Jonathan Cape, London, 1969

Page 57 'I can imagine…remembering': Ben Lerner, *Leaving the Atocha Station*, Coffee House Press, Minneapolis, 2011

Page 59 'each word is…sign': Quotes and paraphrases regarding Funes are from Jorge Luis Borges, 'Funes the Memorious', trans. James E. Irby, *Labyrinths*, Penguin, Melbourne, 2011

Page 63 'You remember too…down': Carson, 'The Glass Essay', *Glass, Irony and God*, New Directions, New York, 1995

Page 73 'You'd be doing…remember': Paraphrase of Cicero, *De oratore*

'False nostalgia'

Page 77 '*Sempre caro mi…colle*': Translations of Leopardi's poems, unless otherwise indicated, are by Jonathan Galassi, *Canti*, Farrar, Straus and Giroux, New York, 2010

Page 78 'sad mood originating…land': Johannes Hofer

(1688) quoted in Svetlana Boym, *The Future of Nostalgia*, Basic Books, New York, 2001

Page 87 'You say *sorry*…awful?': English subtitles of Haneke's script are by Simon John, 2004

Page 89 'Despair is much…boredom': Translations of Leopardi's prose are from Michael Caesar and Franco D'Intino's edition of the *Zibaldone*, Penguin Books, Melbourne, 2013

Page 89 Calvino: 'Exactitude', *Six Memos for the Next Millennium*, trans. Patrick Creagh, Harvard University Press, Cambridge, Mass., 1988

Page 91 'I want at…clarification.': Proust, *The Way by Swann's*

Page 91 'How shall I…back.': *Canti*, trans. J.G. Nichols, Oneworld Classics, Richmond, Surrey, 2008

Page 92 Calvino: 'Exactitude'

Page 93 'reality takes shape…flowers': Proust, *The Way by Swann's*

Page 93 'Over and above the remembering': *Zibaldone*

Page 93 'photos capture people…photo': Paraphrase of John Jeremiah Sullivan, 'Getting Down to What Is Really Real', *Pulphead*, Farrar, Straus and Giroux, New York, 2011

Page 94 'taking pictures of…we're now.': Don DeLillo, *White Noise*, Elisabeth Sifton Books, New York, 1985

Page 119 Weinberger: 'Matteo Ricci'

Acknowledgments

Poems in this collection have previously appeared in *The Age*, *Australian Book Review*, *Australian Poetry Journal*, *Best Australian Poems 2011*, *Best Australian Poems 2013*, *Best Australian Poetry 2009*, *Cordite Poetry Review*, *Jean Cecily Drake-Brockman Poetry Prize 2013 Anthology*, *Melbourne Historical Journal*, *Muse*, *Overland*, *Queensland Poetry Festival 2013 Anthology* and *small wonder*. 'Mountainousness' and 'Ungainly' were featured in *Overland*'s Emerging Poets Series in 2012 and 'Think, again' was also published in the Queensland Poetry Festival e-news.

My thanks go to the editors of these publications, in particular Keri Glastonbury, who published the first of what would become this volume, as well as Gig Ryan, Peter Minter, John Tranter, Alan Wearne and Lisa Gorton.

Special thanks to the guiding hands of Ross Gibson, Stephen Muecke and the late Martin Harrison, without whom this book would not exist. Thanks to Astrid Lorange for her astute and honest feedback, to Alanna Lorenzon for the incomparable cover artwork, to Keir Wotherspoon for introducing false nostalgia to the academy, to Timea Partos for humouring us. To Rebecca Giggs, Pat Grant and Alicia Rodden, for enduring much hand-wringing over the years, and to Claire Hargreave, for her love, patience and conditional approval.

Lastly, thanks to the editors, Fiona Wright and Alice Grundy, and to Ivor Indyk.

This project has been assisted by the Commonwealth Government through the Australia Council for the Arts, its arts funding and advisory body, and by Varuna, The Writers' House.